Donated by
Tara Kowasic

February, 1991

I'm glad I'm me

Illustrated by Mike Higgs

Written by Sally McNulty

© 1984 Rourke Enterprises, Inc.
© 1984 Mike Higgs

Published by Rourke Enterprises, Inc., P.O. Box 3328, Vero Beach, Florida 32964. Copyright © 1984 by Rourke Enterprises, Inc. All copyrights reserved. No part of this book may be reproduced in any form without written permission from the publisher. Printed in the United States of America.

Library of Congress Cataloging in Publication Data

Higgs, Mike, 1945-
  I'm glad I'm me.

  (Learn with Moonbird)
  Summary: Charlie desires to be something or someone else until Moonbird points out all the reasons he has to feel lucky just as he is.
  1. Self-acceptance—Juvenile literature.
  2. Self-perception—Juvenile literature.
  [1. Self-acceptance. 2. Self-perception] I. Title.
  II. Series: Higgs, Mike, 1945-   Learn with Moonbird.
  BF575.S37H54 1984   158'.1   84-16032
  ISBN 0 86592 680 8

ROURKE ENTERPRISES, INC.
Vero Beach, Florida 32964

Charlie and Moonbird were looking for something to do. It was all quiet at Charlie's house. Charlie's mother and little sister were out shopping. "Let's go up to the attic," said Charlie, "It is my secret room."

"I like to imagine things up here," said Charlie. "The family trunk is full of old clothes and toys. I come up here when I'm tired of being me."

Charlie looked into an old mirror. "I'm tired of being me today," he said. "I wish I were somebody else."
"Who do you want to be?" asked Moonbird.

"I wish I were a bird, high in the sky. Then I could fly," said Charlie.

"Birds sometimes fall out of the trees. They are cold in the winter," said Moonbird.

"I wish I were a fish in the sea. A fish in the sea has more fun than me," said Charlie. "That may be, but big fish chase little fish, and little fish must run and hide," said Moonbird. "A fish is not the best thing to be."

"If I were a crocodile, I could live in the jungle. I would have adventures," said Charlie.

"If you were a crocodile, you would have too many teeth to keep clean," said Moonbird. "You have enough teeth to brush just the way you are."

"I will be a hippo and never take a bath," said Charlie.

"Hippos love baths — mud baths!" said Moonbird. "If you were a hippo, you would be dirty forever after. That's a long time."

"I think I'll be a caterpillar and turn into a butterfly," said Charlie.

"You will have nothing but green leaves to eat all day," said Moonbird. "You will miss your milk and cookies."

"I've got it," said Charlie. "I won't be an animal. I will be another person. I will be like Chris. He has twenty friends. I want to have as many friends as he has."

"Your friends are good friends, even if you do not have as many as Chris," said Moonbird. "It is best to have good friends who will stick by you."

"I would like to be rich, like Russ. He can buy whatever he wants," said Charlie.

"Russ is rich, but his mother and father are never home when he needs them. You have a family that loves you," said Moonbird. "Love is more important than money."

"I wish I were a great runner. I would be a star," said Charlie.

"You can do something just as good. You can play the trumpet," said Moonbird. "Didn't you win a prize in music last year?"

"I played in the school band," said Charlie. "That was fun."

"You see," said Moonbird. "You can do something special."

"What else can you do?" Moonbird asked Charlie.
"I can spell," said Charlie.
"That's pretty good," said Moonbird.

"What else can you do?" asked Moonbird.
"I can swim," said Charlie.

"I'm sure that's not all you can do," said Moonbird.
"I can ride a bike," said Charlie.

"I just thought of something I can do that nobody else can do," said Charlie.
"What's that?" asked Moonbird.
"I can wiggle my ears . . . and whistle at the same time!" said Charlie.

"I don't know anyone who can do that," said Moonbird.
"You know me," said Charlie. "Let me think about what else I can do. I can blow bubbles as big as my face."

"I can walk on the wall without falling off," said Charlie. "I can roller skate around the block."

"I collect things, too. I have cards, comics, marbles and erasers in my room," said Charlie.

"You do a lot of things, Charlie," said Moonbird. "You should be glad to be you." "When you put it that way, I guess I am glad to be me," said Charlie.

"I think my mother and sister have come home," said Charlie. "Let's go downstairs and see. I bet everybody doesn't have a funny little sister like I have."

Charlie's mother was fixing milk and cookies. "Would you like some, boys?" she asked.
"That sounds great," said Moonbird and Charlie.

"Your Mom's okay," said Moonbird.
"Yes she is," said Charlie. "I'm pretty lucky to be me."